Redneck EXTREME MOBILE HOME MAKEOVER

Jeff Foxworthy

With illustrations by
David Boyd

RUTLEDGE HILL PRESS
Nashville, Tennessee

A Division of Thomas Nelson Publishers
Since 1798

www.thomasnelson.com

Published by Rutledge Hill Press, a Division of Thomas Nelson, Inc., P.O. Box 141000, Nashville, Tennessee 37214.

Rutledge Hill Press books may be purchased in bulk for educational, business, fundraising, or sales promotional use. For information, please e-mail SpecialMarkets@ThomasNelson.com.

Library of Congress Cataloging-in-Publication Data

Foxworthy, Jeff.
   Redneck extreme mobile home makeover / Jeff Foxworthy ; illustrations by David Boyd.
     p. cm.
   ISBN 1-4016-0225-8 (pbk.)
    1. Rednecks—Humor. 2. Mobile homes—Humor. I. Title.
PN6231.R38F686 2005
818'.5402—dc22   2005017956

Printed in the United States of America

05 06 07 08 09 — 5 4 3 2

Introduction

Extreme home makeover shows have been hugely popular on television recently, but I have found that many rednecks are puzzled by this. As one explained to me, "If you don't like the way your yard looks, you can just hook up your house to the back of your truck and move it, provided none of the tires are flat. And if you don't like the way the inside looks, just wait and the next tornado will probably rearrange it."

Other rednecks I've interviewed about the extreme makeover shows question the judgment of the on-air experts:

"One fellow had installed a screen door on his bathroom so he could keep talking with his buddies while he did his business. I thought that was a great idea, but those fancy-pants designers ripped that sucker right off the hinges."

"There wasn't nothing wrong with that sofa they had in the living room. I mean, it came out of a top-of-the-line Chevy and didn't even have no cigarette burns in it."

"I thought it was real nice having those live plants in all the windows. What difference did it make that they was growing in from the outside instead of being in pots?"

"In my opinion, them TV folks just ruint that house. I'll guarantee you one dang thing—they won't make mine over, 'cause every time I leave the house, I'm taking the front-door steps with me!"

So if you're wondering if maybe your mobile home is a candidate for an extreme makeover, keep a count as you read through the following pages. If more than a dozen of these lines apply to your home, you may want to load the steps in the back of the truck next time you leave.

Jeff Foxworthy

3

You Might Be a Redneck If . . .

Your front yard is on more than one prayer list.

☆

You have a Bud Light pool-table light
hanging over your dining room table.

☆

Hail hits your house and you have to take it
to the body shop for an estimate.

☆

Your security system is the latch on your screen door.

☆

All your home electronics have the serial numbers
filed off.

☆

You've unstopped a sink with a shotgun.

You Might Be a Redneck If . . .

You think a Web site is that corner in your kitchen near the ceiling.

You Might Be a Redneck If . . .

The Orkin man tells you, "Give up! You've lost."

☆

Your daughter's Barbie Dream House
has a clothesline in the front yard.

☆

Any of your front room furniture is inflatable.

☆

Your outdoor light used to be in a mall parking lot.

☆

You get new yard furniture every time the creek floods.

☆

The crack in your toilet seat is named in a lawsuit.

You Might Be a Redneck If . . .

A tree falls through your roof and you decide to leave it.

You Might Be a Redneck If . . .

The flood history of your area can be seen on your living room walls.

You Might Be a Redneck If . . .

Your best china traces the career of Loretta Lynn.

☆

Tidying your yard involves calling a tow truck.

☆

You received rattraps as a wedding present.

☆

You've ever carved a turkey with hedge clippers.

☆

There are hubcap wind chimes anywhere on your block.

☆

Your house doesn't have curtains but your truck does.

You Might Be a Redneck If . . .

You prominently display a gift
you bought at Graceland.

You Might Be a Redneck If . . .

There are more than six vehicles under tarps in your yard.

☆

Your central heating system consists
of leaving the oven door open.

☆

You think people with grass in their yards are uppity.

☆

The diploma hanging in your den includes the words
"Trucking Institute."

☆

Your coffee table is also a cooler.

☆

Your answering machine message begins,
"If you're calling about the free puppies . . ."

You Might Be a Redneck If . . .

Your old bed is now the kids' trampoline.

☆

You refer to your beer gut as "the old tool shed."

☆

All of your kids' toys came free with hamburgers.

☆

You've ever peed your name in the snow.

☆

Getting a package from the post office
requires a full tank of gas in the truck.

☆

You think you're from a "broken home"
because the AC and shower never work.

Your dog
doubles
as your
dishwasher.

You Might Be a Redneck If . . .

Your lawnmower says, "Moo."

☆

Your toenail clippers say Craftsman on the side.

☆

It's impossible to pick up your key chain with just one hand.

☆

You've ever barbecued Spam on the grill.

☆

Nothing in your refrigerator was purchased at a store.

☆

You wonder how service stations
keep their restrooms so clean.

You Might Be a Redneck If . . .

You've ever made a Christmas wreath out of a tire.

You think millennium is what goes on your mama's kitchen floor.

You Might Be a Redneck If . . .

Your chest of drawers used to be a roll-around toolbox.

☆

You've ever used a shop vac to vacuum your pool.

☆

There are crawfish in your home aquarium.

☆

You've stolen turf from a golf course.

☆

When you say, "Let's hit the hay," you mean it literally.

☆

You have two big-screen TVs, but no running water.

You can tell your car is low on oil
by looking at the garage floor.

You Might Be a Redneck If . . .

You dye your hair and clean your floors with the same stuff.

☆

You've ever relieved yourself in the neighbor's yard.

☆

Directions to your house include
"turn off the paved road."

☆

You think a stock tip is advice on wormin' your hogs.

☆

Your mailman wears a bee net and snake boots.

☆

You have separate mortgages on your home
and the land it's parked on.

You Might Be a Redneck If . . .

Your shotgun sees more action than your lawn mower.

☆

The neighbors refer to your doublewide on a sand mound
as "the mansion on the hill."

☆

Most of the stuff in your garage doesn't belong to you.

☆

Your ATM is your mattress.

☆

You think a whistling teakettle is high tech.

☆

You spray-painted your dead shrubbery green.

You Might Be a Redneck If . . .

You have an aboveground swimming pool
that you fish out of.

You Might Be a Redneck If . . .

You've ever used the kids' swing set as a clothesline.

☆

Your bridal veil was made of window screen.

☆

The original color of your carpet is an unsolved mystery.

☆

There is a hot tub in your living room.

☆

Your dog's bed is a pile of dirty clothes.

☆

Your smoke detector doubles as your dinner bell.

You Might Be a Redneck If . . .

Your backyard grill used to be
a rest-stop trash can.

Your car and your house
are both up on blocks.

You Might Be a Redneck If . . .

You have to drive through three gates
to get to your house.

☆

Every decoration in your living room relates to NASCAR.

☆

Your burps set off smoke detectors.

☆

Making love by candlelight is the only option
you have after dark.

☆

You've taken a "Velvet Elvis" for an insurance appraisal.

☆

Your gazebo is an old satellite dish held up by PVC pipes.

You Might Be a Redneck If . . .

Your birdhouse used to be
a Clorox bottle.

You Might Be a Redneck If . . .

The garbage truck mistakenly takes your lawn furniture.

☆

Your toilet tissue is Taco Bell napkins.

☆

Your Christmas ornaments are hung with paper clips.

☆

The phone number for a pizza delivery company
is written on the wall above your phone.

☆

Your yard gets mistaken for a petting zoo.

☆

You open your walk-in beer cooler with a Clapper.

You Might Be a Redneck If . . .

Your air conditioner is louder than your TV.

☆

You have the entire WWF Slurpee cup collection proudly
displayed on a shelf in your trailer.

☆

The only time you empty your ashtray is when
you knock it over.

☆

Your neighbors think you are a detective because
a cop always brings you home.

☆

The bloodmobile will not visit your trailer park.

☆

You've ever nailed your Christmas tree to the floor.

You've ever used jumper cables
to start your computer.

You Might Be a Redneck If . . .

You have to mow around a refrigerator and a bed frame.

☆

The man from the power company threatens
to cut off your service, and you threaten
to cut off something of his in return.

☆

You've ever cleaned your brake drums in the dishwasher.

☆

The ATF has an interest in your storage unit.

☆

You're raising one species of animal as food for another.

☆

You price everything really high at your yard sale in
hopes that no one will buy it.

You've ever served Christmas dinner
on a Ping-Pong table.

You Might Be a Redneck If . . .

There is a Jack Daniel's poster in your living room.

☆

You've ever committed a crime with a lawn mower.

☆

You keep catfish in your aquarium.

☆

Your mounted deer head sports
a baseball cap and sunglasses.

☆

A different cat sleeps on your head every night.

☆

Your address is spray-painted on your front door.

You get a clear picture
only when the cat sits on the TV.

You Might Be a Redneck If . . .

Someone knocks on your front door
and your back door rattles.

☆

Your family tree has a tire swing.

☆

The graffiti on your fence is in your handwriting.

☆

Your screen door keeps more bugs in than out.

☆

You've ever tried to go down your porch steps
on a pogo stick.

☆

Your idea of lawn maintenance
is a can of gasoline and a lighter.

You Might Be a Redneck If . . .

You've used a casserole dish as a footbath.

☆

Your "second home" is actually a storage unit.

☆

Bill collectors carpool to your home.

☆

Property downwind from your home is virtually worthless.

☆

Breakfast every morning is interrupted by someone
asking, "Anybody seen my teeth?"

☆

You have Pabst Blue Ribbon
on tap anywhere in your house.

You Might Be a Redneck If . . .

The only cordless phone you have is the one your wife ripped out of the wall when she caught you talking to your girlfriend.

You Might Be a Redneck If . . .

There's no mirror in your bathroom.

☆

You've ever used hair spray to kill flying bugs.

☆

You have a relative living in your garage.

☆

The oil stain in your driveway is bigger than your car.

☆

You've ever changed the numbers on your house
so the police couldn't find you.

☆

You owe more to Blockbuster Video
than you do on your house.

You Might Be a Redneck If . . .

Turning on your lights involves pulling a string.

You Might Be a Redneck If . . .

Your riding lawn mower has cup holders.

You Might Be a Redneck If . . .

Your alarm clock has only one hand.

☆

The trunk of your car doubles as a deep freeze.

☆

You can play "Sweet Home Alabama"
on your touch-tone phone.

☆

You practice your duck calls at the dinner table.

☆

There's a hole in the ozone layer directly above your house.

☆

You've ever walked through the living room and
caught your neck in a clothesline.

You Might Be a Redneck If . . .

There are more dishes in your sink
than in your cabinets.

You Might Be a Redneck If . . .

You have a bug light inside your house.

☆

Your home phone is three blocks away in a booth.

☆

The local gun and knife show is held in your basement.

☆

Your bowling trophies are insured.

☆

The pizza delivery man won't come to your house
without bringing the police with him.

☆

You've lived in the same house at five different addresses.

You Might Be a Redneck If . . .

The most common phrase heard in your house
is "Somebody go jiggle the handle!"

☆

You've ever experienced road rage in your own driveway.

☆

Your spare key is a chain saw.

☆

The welcome wagon was scared to stop at your house.

☆

You've ever had sex in a satellite dish.

☆

Your front yard looks like Toys "R" Us after a tornado.

You've ever raked leaves
in your own kitchen.

You Might Be a Redneck If . . .

Your wife's laundry basket used to be a grocery cart.

☆

There is a stuffed possum mounted
anywhere in your home.

☆

You can entertain yourself for more than
an hour with a flyswatter.

☆

Your garbage man is confused about
what goes and what stays.

☆

Neighborhood kids knock on your door as a dare.

☆

You actually wear the shoes your dog brings home.

You Might Be a Redneck If . . .

You've ever driven around looking for your porch roof after a bad storm.

You Might Be a Redneck If . . .

Your electrical outlet is a safety hazard.

☆

You clean your house with a water hose.

☆

Realtors refuse to sell your home.

☆

You've tightened a loose screw with your fingernail.

☆

Your front yard doubles as a go-cart track.

☆

The box your TV came in has also served as a clubhouse,
a laundry basket, and a playpen.

You Might Be a Redneck If . . .

When it rains, there are more pots and pans in your living room than in your kitchen.

You Might Be a Redneck If . . .

Your exercise bike is currently on blocks.

☆

You secretly get your firewood from your neighbor's yard.

☆

The plastic deer in your yard
are not decorations—they're practice targets.

☆

Your basketball hoop is a fishing net.

☆

At least one corner of your bed is supported by a tire.

☆

You think "hiding your valuables" means putting the
Nutter Butter cookies under the couch.

You Might Be a Redneck If . . .

Your richest relative buys a new house
and you have to help take the wheels off.

☆

You've ever hollered,
"You kids quit playing on that sheet metal!"

☆

The curtains in your living room are camouflage.

☆

You have 16 cats living in your yard
but can't get close enough to pet any of them.

☆

You use a piece of bread as a napkin.

☆

Your neighbor has ever asked to borrow a quart of beer.

You Might Be a Redneck If . . .

You keep a can of Raid on your kitchen table.

☆

There's a belch on your answering machine greeting.

☆

Your toilet paper has page numbers on it.

☆

You have a lava lamp over five feet tall.

☆

Your dog passes gas and you claim it.

☆

The police come to talk to you about your "tomato" plants.

You Might Be a Redneck If . . .

There are more than 10 cats living under your trailer.

You permanently have someone
staying on your couch.

You Might Be a Redneck If . . .

Your tablecloth was delivered by the paperboy.

☆

You've ever shot dead limbs out
of trees in your front yard.

☆

All you get on your TV is the sound.

☆

You take out a home improvement loan
to buy a new camper shell.

☆

Your aboveground pool is used for storage.

☆

There are eight chairs on your porch,
but none of them is safe to sit on.

You Might Be a Redneck If . . .

You repaint the pink flamingos in the front yard every spring.

You Might Be a Redneck If . . .

You invite all your relatives over
to see your new ceiling fan.

☆

Callers can hear dogs barking
on your answering machine greeting.

☆

Your wife has four-wheel drive on her vacuum cleaner.

☆

There's graffiti on the bathroom wall in your own house.

☆

You think a water bed is a status symbol.

☆

You've ever conducted business while sitting on the toilet.

You Might Be a Redneck If . . .

All your neighbors have electric fences.

☆

Your engine block is cleaner than your stovetop.

☆

You think "haute cuisine"
is after it comes out of the microwave.

☆

Your barn is nicer than your house.

☆

You've ever had a romantic
encounter on a riding lawn mower.

☆

Your pet bunny Fluffy was the hit of Easter morning and
served with sweet potatoes at the Fouth of July picnic.

You Might Be a Redneck If . . .

You clean your garage and realize
that you didn't sell your motorcycle.

You Might Be a Redneck If . . .

Your septic tank is the subject of a petition.

☆

Orkin uses your house as a training site.

☆

You execute holds on your dog
while watching TV wrestling.

☆

There are more clothes on your floors
than in your drawers.

☆

You've reused a "yard sale" sign more than ten times.

☆

You and six of your neighbors split a cable bill.

You Might Be a Redneck If . . .

Your dogs always get to your trash before the garbage truck does.

You Might Be a Redneck If . . .

You've ever watched a tornado from a lawn chair.

You Might Be a Redneck If . . .

You've ever given a full set of NASCAR plastic
cups as a wedding present.

☆

Cleaning out your garage involves a backhoe.

☆

Your motor home used to be a church bus.

☆

Any of your children were conceived on a tire swing.

☆

You've ever framed an *Auto Trader* cover.

☆

You know for a fact that a sock can be used for toilet paper.

You Might Be a Redneck If . . .

You have to go outside
to get something out of the fridge.

You Might Be a Redneck If . . .

Anything in your home is running off a car battery.

☆

You're using your kids' swing set as an engine hoist.

☆

Your mailing address is c/o Waffle House.

☆

The church social committee
is afraid to meet at your house.

☆

You still own every tire you ever bought.

☆

Your brother had to cosign to get your deer mounted.

You Might Be a Redneck If . . .

Your home has ever appeared on a humorous postcard.

☆

You think "prime real estate" is the chair next
to the space heater.

☆

No matter which side of the tracks you live on,
it's the wrong side.

☆

There is more carpet on your toilet than on your floors.

☆

You've never seen the bottom of your kitchen sink.

☆

You married your wife for her socket set.

You Might Be a Redneck If . . .

You've ever clogged your vacuum
with a small animal.

You Might Be a Redneck If . . .

You're still keeping a goldfish
in the plastic bag you won it in.

☆

Going to the bathroom in the middle
of the night requires shoes and a flashlight.

☆

Your prenuptial agreement mentions chickens.

☆

The centerpiece of your landscaping used
to get 25 miles per gallon.

☆

You wet the bed and four other people immediately know it.

☆

You've ever held up someone with a caulk gun.

You Might Be a Redneck If . . .

Your front gate is an iron headboard.

You Might Be a Redneck If . . .

The only big bucks you've ever come into are hanging over your fireplace.

You Might Be a Redneck If . . .

You've ever used panty hose as a coffee filter.

☆

Your living room sofa came out of a Chevrolet.

☆

The diving contest at the family reunion was ruined
because your pool went flat.

☆

You think orange peels left on the coffee table
are potpourri.

☆

Any of your wedding gifts came
from an Army Navy store.

☆

You're saving up to "gravel" your driveway.

The oil stain in your driveway was once a barbecue sandwich.

You Might Be a Redneck If . . .

Your family stays cool by sitting on the porch naked.

☆

Your doorbell is a dog.

☆

Your children catch frogs and lizards . . .
inside the house.

☆

You go to a party and the punch bowl flushes.

☆

Friends see your sunglasses lying on the counter
and their first thought is "Elvis is alive!"

☆

You didn't put the pink plastic flamingos
in your front yard as a joke.

You Might Be a Redneck If . . .

FedEx stops at your house only for directions.

☆

Your landscaping includes corn and squash.

☆

The only private club you've ever belonged to
is Sam's Wholesale Club.

☆

You've ever skinny-dipped in an inflatable pool.

☆

You set your shoes outside and the flowers died.

☆

You view duct tape as a long-term investment.

Your kid's favorite teething ring is the
garden hose in the front yard.

You Might Be a Redneck If . . .

Your children's night-light is a neon beer sign.

☆

Tear gas was ever fired into your trailer.

☆

You pay $1,200 a year to store $300 worth of stuff.

☆

You've ever mixed drinks in an aquarium.

☆

There is a laminated picture of Rambo
on your headboard.

☆

You're using a Twister mat as a shower curtain.

You inherited a stolen road sign.

You Might Be a Redneck If . . .

Your lawn fertilizer was in your cow about five minutes earlier.

You Might Be a Redneck If . . .

You keep a musical instrument in your bathroom.

☆

Your houseguests never stay twice.

☆

You put antlers on top of your Christmas tree
instead of an angel.

☆

The doctor who delivered your children
also delivers your propane.

☆

Your truck has more lights than your house.

☆

You think toilet water is exactly that.

You Might Be a Redneck If . . .

Your front porch collapses and kills more
than three dogs.

☆

You paint your car with house paint.

☆

The Salvation Army declines your mattress.

☆

You didn't have to leave your house
to pick up your date for the prom.

☆

There's a U-Haul truck on blocks in your yard.

☆

Your fishpond used to be your hot tub.

You Might Be a Redneck If . . .

Your RV is bigger than your house.

☆

The only pool you've ever owned is a cesspool.

☆

You move your couch and find 14 cigarette lighters,
$1.37 in change, and a six-year-old *TV Guide.*

☆

Your most expensive piece of art is held up
with thumbtacks.

☆

You buy stuff at your own yard sale.

☆

There are orange road cones in your living room.

The "Save Naugahyde" protection group chooses your house as a picket site.

You Might Be a Redneck If . . .

Your landscaping features cattle skulls.

☆

You've ever used a cheese ball as a weapon.

☆

You enjoy full cable TV service when your neighbor
leaves his curtains open.

☆

The shower runs cold when your neighbor
flushes his commode.

☆

You've ever hunted within 20 yards
of your child's swing set.

☆

You get poison ivy, chigger bites,
and fleas just walking to your mailbox.

You Might Be a Redneck If . . .

People drive from miles away
to look at your grandma's underpants
hanging on the clothesline.

You Might Be a Redneck If . . .

You've ever jacked up your home to look for a dog.

You Might Be a Redneck If . . .

You've ever videotaped a yard sale.

☆

The strongest smell in your house is butane.

☆

Your sneeze can disrupt TV reception.

☆

You grow your own chewing tobacco.

☆

The house feels a bit lonely when winter comes
and the last fly dies.

☆

Your tools are worth more than your car.

You Might Be a Redneck If . . .

You know that your wheelbarrow will hold ten 12-packs iced down.

You Might Be a Redneck If . . .

You can't remember where your lawn mower is.

☆

The dogcatcher calls for backup when he goes
to your house.

☆

You vacuum the sheets instead of washing them.

☆

You've ever used a bathtub as a punch bowl.

☆

Your yard has more than 10 ceramic figurines.

☆

You have your appendix in a jar sitting on your mantel,
with the track lighting focused on it.

You Might Be a Redneck If . . .

You've ever cleaned fish in your living room.

☆

One of the blankets on your bed says
"Property of U-Haul."

☆

Your doghouse and your living room
have the same shag carpet.

☆

You think Rolex is bathroom tissue.

☆

You have a family portrait drawn by a courtroom artist.

☆

Your wife has ever said,
"Come move this transmission so I can take a bath."

You Might Be a Redneck If . . .

You flush the toilet and the dog thinks
you're giving him fresh water.

You Might Be a Redneck If . . .

You've ever caught bugs just so you could
throw them in the bug-zapper.

☆

Your mother keeps a spit cup on the ironing board.

☆

The deer head over your fireplace
is wearing your Mardi Gras beads.

☆

You know more than a dozen uses for old tires.

☆

You've ever had to have a wrecker pull your car out
of a pothole in your driveway.

☆

The Roto-Rooter man comes to your house and asks,
"What's that smell?"

You Might Be a Redneck If . . .

The neighbors call 911 every time you use the barbecue grill.

You Might Be a Redneck If . . .

Your dream home is stuck in traffic.

☆

Every time you move, the neighbors throw a party.

☆

Your sofa used to be a weight bench.

☆

There are cuss words on your answering machine greeting.

☆

You have a tire swing in your house.

☆

Your yard has ever been the proposed site for a landfill.

You don't have electricity
in every room of your house.

You Might Be a Redneck If . . .

Your chicken house used to be a school bus.

☆

You tie down the furniture in the back of your truck
with a garden hose.

☆

There is a ham hanging from your front porch.

☆

You were registered at the Everything's a Dollar store.

☆

Auto salvage yards regard you as competition.

☆

You rebuilt a carburetor while sitting on the commode.

You Might Be a Redneck If . . .

Your workbench used to be your front door.

☆

You've ever repaired a broken vase with Polygrip.

☆

Your bathroom has a different
mailing address than your house.

☆

You use a bedsheet as a sofa cover.

☆

Your wife sleeps on the couch
every time you eat at Taco Bell.

☆

You stop and pick up furniture others have thrown out.

You have to honk your horn
when pulling into your driveway
to keep from killing chickens.

You Might Be a Redneck If . . .

You have a CB radio in your bathroom.

☆

You've mixed cement in a clothes dryer.

☆

Making your bed involves moving at least three animals.

☆

You steal the towels when you stay overnight with relatives.

☆

Your chili's secret ingredient comes from the bait shop.

☆

There's a grave in your yard.

You removed your bathroom door so you could watch TV from the commode.

You Might Be a Redneck If . . .

Your mail is delivered every other Thursday.

☆

There's an expired license plate hanging
on your living room wall.

☆

You've ever used duct tape to repair dental work.

☆

You have Mason jars filled
with stuff the FBI can't identify.

☆

Starting your car wakes at least 12 cats.

☆

Your TV gets 512 channels,
but you have to go outside to use the bathroom.

You Might Be a Redneck If . . .

The morning after your last party, you woke up in the bathtub.

You Might Be a Redneck If . . .

You are famous in your neighborhood for your bonfires.

☆

You made a homemade hot tub with a trolling motor.

☆

Your Thanksgiving centerpiece has ever been prepared
by a taxidermist.

☆

You've ever shot a deer from inside your house.

☆

You're naked on laundry day.

☆

You think "neighborhood watch" is what your
mother-in-law does on the porch all day.

You Might Be a Redneck If . . .

You've ever tried to fix car dents
with a bathroom plunger.

☆

Your mailbox holds up one end of your clothesline.

☆

You've ever confused a bread pan with a bedpan.

☆

While duckwalking to get a new roll of toilet paper, you
stumble into your wife's Bible study meeting.

☆

You are famous for your homemade squash wine.

☆

Your retirement plans include getting your own place.

Your idea of an exciting time is throwing a piece of meat out into the yard and watching the dogs fight over it.

You Might Be a Redneck If . . .

You think a love seat is the one on the passenger's side.

☆

Your dog has ever brought home something
that you cooked for dinner.

☆

You've used Pam for shoe polish.

☆

Your toilet is up on blocks.

☆

Privacy in your bathroom means singing loudly.

☆

Your burglar alarm is a vacuum cleaner plugged
into a motion detector.

Your Christmas
tree has a deer
stand in it.

You Might Be a Redneck If . . .

Your property has been mistaken
for a recycling center.

You Might Be a Redneck If . . .

Your satellite dish has more square footage than your home.

☆

You paint your garage with a paintball gun.

☆

You've bandaged a wound with duct tape.

☆

You're on a first name basis with animal control.

☆

The fire that burned your yard up was started
with a bottle rocket.

☆

You have no hubcaps on your car because you're using
them to feed your hunting dogs.

You Might Be a Redneck If . . .

Your old washing machine
is your new doghouse.

You Might Be a Redneck If . . .

You broke even at your last yard sale.

☆

Your trailer has an ornamental fountain out front.

☆

The hardest part of your divorce was dividing up your
shot glass collection.

☆

You've ever cooked in WD-40.

☆

Police ever opened your front door with a battering ram.

☆

You've cut down a tree so you could
watch the neighbors better.

You Might Be a Redneck If . . .

You think NSYNC is where your dirty dishes are.

☆

You've ever fixed your false teeth with a glue gun.

☆

The only running water in your home
is leaking through the ceiling.

☆

Your truck, car, boat, and mower
all share the same battery.

☆

Your favorite suntan lotion is Crisco.

☆

You think a lavatory is a breed of dog.

You've ever moved furniture in a horse trailer.

☆

Everything in your icebox smells like deer meat.

☆

Your TV's remote control is your son Junior.

☆

Your wife has a Jell-O mold that looks like Elvis.

☆

You have bumper stickers on your riding mower.

☆

The second thing you say after answering the phone is
"Sitting around, drinking beer."

You Might Be a Redneck If . . .

Your kids' swing set has been condemned.

Any of your
furniture has
bullet holes.

You Might Be a Redneck If . . .

You've asked for layaway at the Dollar Store.

☆

The lawn-care service never leaves
a flyer on your front door.

☆

You need pliers to change the channel on your TV.

☆

You've ever worked in your garden with a kitchen fork.

☆

You often find stray animals in your living room.

☆

Your wife's jewelry box plays
"Beast of Burden" when opened.

You Might Be a Redneck If . . .

Your home security system features fishing twine and tin cans.

You Might Be a Redneck If . . .

You inherited a toilet plunger.

☆

Your front porch is a tourist attraction.

☆

You regularly answer the door in your underwear,
carrying a baseball bat.

☆

Your dog has his own recliner.

☆

There is a tree growing out of a car in your yard.

☆

Your lawn mowers are named Nanny and Billy.

You Might Be a Redneck If . . .

Your car and its motor are more than ten feet apart.

☆

There is a trampoline in your front yard.

☆

You own all the components of soap-on-a-rope
except the soap.

☆

You've ever made a cup of coffee with a welding torch.

☆

Your mobile home has a loft.

☆

You think "home security" means taking the front steps
to your trailer with you when you leave the house.

You Might Be a Redneck If . . .

There's no screen in your screen door.

You Might Be a Redneck If . . .

Your plumbing makes poltergeist noises.

☆

You think *Silence of the Lambs* is what happens when somebody walks toward the barn.

☆

At least one dog slept in your bed on your wedding night.

☆

You have a fence in your yard, but it's not up.

☆

You get your mail sent to a P.O. box because you can't spell or pronounce your street name.

☆

You think "wireless communication" means yelling across your front yard.

You Might Be a Redneck If . . .

Your hairstylist also cuts your grass.

☆

The engine hanging in your yard
is newer than the one in your car.

☆

Your house catches on fire and you run back
in to save the deer heads.

☆

You can get your arm to the bottom of a full box of cereal.

☆

Your three-year-old is trained to bring a beer
to any cops that show up at the door.

☆

There's a cardboard cutout of Dale Earnhardt
in your living room.

You Might Be a Redneck If . . .

Your bathroom towels are also
your bathroom curtains.

You Might Be a Redneck If . . .

Your mailbox is made out of old auto parts.

☆

All the art in your living room was purchased
at gas stations.

☆

Your pocketknife doubles as a toenail clipper
and a cheese slicer.

☆

Putting your dog to sleep involves a warm bowl
of milk and a bedtime story.

☆

Your house has ever been involved in a traffic accident.

☆

You think "the dishwasher is broke"
means your wife has no money.

You Might Be a Redneck If . . .

There's an endangered species in your freezer.

☆

You think four-on-the-floor is a sleeping arrangement.

☆

The only upholstered seat
in your home is on the commode.

☆

You videotape fishing shows.

☆

In preparation for your upcoming wedding,
you register your Tupperware pattern.

☆

Your dog buries bones in the middle of your living room.

You Might Be a Redneck If . . .

Your porch swing is a tire swing.

You Might Be a Redneck If . . .

You think the phrase "chicken out"
means one of your pets has escaped.

☆

Grass is growing in the floorboards of your car.

☆

Your TV is on 24/7.

☆

You've ever waved at traffic from your front porch wearing nothing but your underwear.

☆

You use your bathroom plunger every day.

☆

Your idea of conservation is moving your Saturday night
bath to every other Saturday night.

You use a hubcap
as an ashtray.

You Might Be a Redneck If . . .

You have a front door
but no steps to get to it.

You Might Be a Redneck If . . .

You have a framed portrait of a hog.

☆

Your wife got Caller ID so she'd know
which bar you're in.

☆

The seats on your porch used to be seats in your car.

☆

You like to take your own mattress along on a trip.

☆

There are four pairs of pants and two squirrels
hanging from your clothesline.

☆

You buy brown sheets so you don't have to wash them.

You Might Be a Redneck If . . .

Your living room curtains are beach towels.

☆

The only diploma on your wall is from DUI school.

☆

The neighbors started a petition over your Christmas lights.

☆

Your kids can't use the sandbox because the cats do.

☆

You've been photographed with a prize-winning vegetable.

☆

Strangers knock on your door mistakenly
thinking you're having a yard sale.

You Might Be a Redneck If . . .

The slipcover on your sofa used to be a shower curtain.

☆

You can name more than six brands of chain saws.

☆

Your dogs sleep on your bed and your wife
sleeps on the sofa.

☆

The nearest liquor store is brewing in your basement.

☆

Your toothbrush is a hand-me-down.

☆

You have a full set of salad bowls
that all say Cool Whip on the side of them.

Your bathroom deodorizer
is a box of kitchen matches.

You Might Be a Redneck If . . .

You've ever taken a deer skin to the dry cleaners.

☆

The local police go on alert during your Super Bowl party.

☆

There is a four-wheeler parked in your bedroom.

☆

Your will is written on a Post-it note.

☆

The only things not rusted in your yard are the pinwheels
on either side of the driveway.

☆

You think your dog is "house trained" because
that is the only place he will go.

Your kids trip over the Christmas lights
while hunting Easter eggs.

You Might Be a Redneck If . . .

Your houseplants aren't in pots.

You Might Be a Redneck If . . .

Your TV is a big screen if you use your binoculars.

☆

You think a doubleheader is an outhouse with two seats.

☆

You've ever picked birdshot out of your fried chicken.

☆

You cut your toenails in front of company.

☆

Every time the wind blows, you find shingles in your yard.

☆

You regularly check the brake lights on your house.

You've ever misspelled anything
in Christmas lights.

You Might Be a Redneck If . . .

You had your trailer bricked in.

☆

Blowing a tire means a new flowerpot for the front yard.

☆

You've ever been third through the bath water.

☆

You've tried to dry underwear in a microwave.

☆

Homegrown tomatoes make your list
of the most important things in life.

☆

You stockpile pork and beans.

You Might Be a Redneck If . . .

Your fence doubles as your clothesline.

☆

The Palmolive you soak your hands
in also has dirty dishes in it.

☆

You have used a potato peeler to remove a corn.

☆

You've ever stood in the yard
in your underwear shouting, "It's Friday!"

☆

The auto junkyard calls you to get spare parts.

☆

You have more things with Hank Williams Jr.'s
name on them than your own.

You Might Be a Redneck If . . .

Your aboveground pool is now your wrestling ring.

☆

You've ever gotten into a fistfight over a Pop-Tart.

☆

The city council ever discussed your front yard.

☆

You disguise your voice when answering the phone.

☆

You've ever plucked a nose hair with a pair of pliers.

☆

The last time you cleaned the ashes out of your fireplace,
Richard Petty didn't know how to drive.

You Might Be a Redneck If . . .

There are hoof prints on your carpet.

You Might Be a Redneck If . . .

Your toolshed has four flats and is missing its transmission.

☆

You know more than 30 ways to prepare Spam.

☆

Drying your clothes depends upon the weather.

☆

You have to wash your hands *before* you go
to the bathroom.

☆

The trash barrel is the focal point of your landscape theme.

☆

You answer all phone calls with "Check's in the mail."

You served your Christmas turkey on a platter bearing Dale Earnhardt's picture.

You Might Be a Redneck If . . .

There's a home theater system in your garage.

☆

You have the cooking instructions
for macaroni and cheese memorized.

☆

Your toothbrush is just that.

☆

You practice casting in your yard.

☆

Your parrot can say, "Open up, it's the police!"

☆

Lighting your deck means pulling the truck around back.

You Might Be a Redneck If . . .

You get carpal tunnel syndrome from the TV remote.

☆

Your wife puts candles on a pan of corn bread
for your birthday.

☆

The post office discontinues your service because the
mailman keeps getting stuck in your driveway.

☆

You use a screwdriver to start your pickup.

☆

You've opened a can of chili with a handgun.

☆

Your deer lease costs more than your house.

You Might Be a Redneck If . . .

There are more things growing in your refrigerator than in your yard.

You Might Be a Redneck If . . .

The chairs in your living room are stackable.

☆

You have a drawerful of ketchup and hot-sauce packets
from fast-food restaurants.

☆

There is an electronic singing fish in more
than three rooms of your house.

☆

Your standard of living improves when you go camping.

☆

You moved into a doublewide to accommodate
your wide-screen TV.

☆

You've ever used a Weed Eater indoors.

You Might Be a Redneck If . . .

You can't remember what the blue tarp in your front yard is covering.

You Might Be a Redneck If . . .

You turn on your sprinkler and tell your kids
it's a water park.

☆

You've ever used a skateboard to move an appliance.

☆

Mosquito Control comes to talk to you about your pool.

☆

Your dog has a litter of puppies
on the living room floor and nobody notices.

☆

Police dust your furniture more often than you do.

☆

Your previous two homes are rotting in the back pasture.